# MARVELLOUS MOBILE PHONES:
## A Manual Accounting Practice Set

## by Mellida Frost

**Marvellous mobile phones: A manual accounting practice set**
**1st Edition**
**Mellida Frost**

Publishing manager: Alison Green
Publishing editor: Gregory Studdert
Project editor: Michaela Skelly
Developmental editor: Meagan Carlsson
Cover design: Miranda Costa
Proofreader: Leanne Poll

Any URLs contained in this publication were checked for currency during the production process. Note, however, that the publisher cannot vouch for the ongoing currency of URLs.

This first edition is printed in 2011

For product information and technology assistance,
in Australia call **1300 790 853**;
in New Zealand call **0800 449 725**

For permission to use material from this text or product, please email
**aust.permissions@cengage.com**

**National Library of Australia Cataloguing-in-Publication Data**
Author: Frost, Mellida.
Title: Marvellous Mobile Phones : a manual accounting practice set / Mellida Frost.
ISBN: 9780170199230 (loose-leaf)
Subjects: Accounting--Textbooks.
Dewey Number: 657

**Cengage Learning Australia**
Level 7, 80 Dorcas Street
South Melbourne, Victoria Australia 3205

**Cengage Learning New Zealand**
Unit 4B Rosedale Office Park
331 Rosedale Road, Albany, North Shore 0632, NZ

For learning solutions, visit **cengage.com.au**

Printed in China by RR Donnelley Asia Printing Solutions Limited.
1 2 3 4 5 6 7 15 14 13 12 11

# Table of contents

# About the author

Mellida has over 16 years experience in account keeping, including preparing the payroll for over 200 employees, maintaining accounting systems and preparing monthly financial and management reports.

The combination of high grades at University (including Commendations from the Board of Examiners) and varied practical accounting experience has resulted in a thorough understanding of the financial accounting process. Her flair for systemising and simplifying administrative and accounting processes has led to a successful small business, specialising in troubleshooting and teaching employees to streamline business processes.

Mellida is in the process of completing her Master of Professional Accounting at Curtin University of Technology. She also teaches at Curtin University of Technology and her teaching responsibilities include MYOB, Quickbooks and Accounting Technologies, as well as preparing tests and administration.

Her ability to teach accounting subjects with zeal has led to student-voted faculty awards for teaching. She is an active participant of a Rostrum club.

# Acknowledgement

The publisher and the author would like to thank Mr Rex Lang from Chisholm Institute for completing a technical edit of this practice set. His feedback and corrections have been crucial to the development of this title.

# CHAPTER 1
# Introduction

## What can I expect from this practice set?

This practice set will guide students through the manual account keeping for a fictitious company called Marvellous Mobile Phones (MMP). This practice set is designed to complement a basic financial accounting unit by providing a 'real life' scenario in which to practice.

It is all well and good to learn the theory in class, but there are many advantages to applying this knowledge to an actual business. Students are encouraged to use logic and critical thinking when performing the tasks, rather than learning by rote. This helps to develop problem-solving skills and confidence.

With all the cheap accounting software available, few businesses actually use strictly manual account-keeping systems. However, a deep understanding of manual account keeping assists the user in ensuring the integrity of the data and enables them to find and correct mistakes.

The author has deliberately used simple words and initial detailed instructions to make this practice set easy to read and work through. Like Sudoku and Addoku, manual account keeping requires the user to arrange numbers according to a set of rules, namely *double-entry accounting*.

On completion, you will know how to do the following tasks:

- Interpret and extract information from source documents.
- Journalise and post transactions to the appropriate journals and ledgers.
- Use multiple Sales and Cost of Goods Sold accounts.
- Record sales invoices, apply sales credits and receive payments from customers.
- Record purchase invoices, apply purchase credits and pay suppliers.
- Account for GST and discounts (both taken and received).
- Maintain Accounts Payable and Accounts Receivable subsidiary ledgers.
- Maintain a perpetual inventory system.
- Record adjustments after a stocktake.
- Prepare a bank reconciliation.
- Process petty cash.
- Pay and record wages in the most basic form, including PAYG Withholding tax.
- Pay and record liabilities such as superannuation, loans, GST and PAYG Withholding.
- Process depreciation and bad and doubtful debts.
- Process reversing, adjusting and closing journal entries.
- Prepare useful financial reports.

# Goods and Services Tax (GST)

One of the most common mistakes made by students is the incorrect recording of the Goods and Services Tax (GST). For the purposes of this practice set, all you need to know is that GST is 10% of the normal income and most expenses of the business. As such, it does not form part of the profit and loss.

A business only needs to register for GST if the turnover is greater than a threshold set by the Australian Taxation Office (ATO). In 20X1, the turnover threshold is $75,000 for businesses and $150,000 for not-for-profit organisations.

GST is charged on the provision of goods and services. If you provide a service (i.e. you are a lawyer and provide legal services), you are required to charge your client an extra 10% tax, which is remitted to the tax department with a business activity statement (BAS). The same applies if you are selling goods (such as furniture or pet food). There are some exceptions to the requirement to charge GST. These include 'necessities' such as milk, water and bread.

Some business people complain about paying GST, thinking that it is another tax that the business has to pay, such as income tax. This is not the case. The business is still receiving the income it would normally receive from the customer. However, the business needs to charge an extra 10% that is remitted (paid) to the ATO. So effectively it is the customer that bears the burden of the tax.

For example, if a business normally charges an Australian customer $1000.00 for providing a service, it then has to add 10% tax ($100.00). This tax is put into a liability account because the business 'owes' the tax to the Australian Taxation Office (ATO).

| Normal charge | 1000.00 | Post to an income account |
|---|---|---|
| GST of 10% | 100.00 | Post to a liability account called GST Collected. |
| Total cost to customer | 1100.00 | Post to accounts receivable |

The business can also claim GST credits for expenses of the business. These credits are offset against the GST Liability and effectively reduce the amount due to the ATO.

| Total price of expense | 550.00 | Post to accounts payable |
|---|---|---|
| GST credits of 10% included in that cost | 50.00 | Post to an asset account called GST Paid |
| Real cost to the business | 500.00 | Post to expense account |

Some terms that are used in connection with GST are shown in Table 1.1.

| Term | Definition |
|---|---|
| GST inclusive | The final price of the good or service including the GST (has the GST already in the price). |
| GST exclusive | The cost of the good or service excluding the GST (GST of 10% needs to be added on to arrive at the dollar amount to be paid or charged). |
| GST free | An exception to the GST rule where no GST is charged. Examples include milk, coffee beans and donations. |
| Non-reportable | The expense or transaction does not involve a good or service and so is not subject to GST. Examples include transfer of money between bank accounts, owner drawings, wages and superannuation. |

Table 1.1    *Accounting terms used throughout the practice set*

To arrive at a GST-*in*clusive amount when you are only given a GST-*ex*clusive amount, multiply that amount by 10% to get the GST figure and add it on.

| | | |
|---|---|---|
| GST *ex*clusive amount | 200.00 | Amount in income or expense account |
| *Plus* 10% of 200.00 | + 20.00 | Amount in GST account |
| = GST-*in*clusive amount | 220.00 | Total paid out or received by the business |

To arrive at a GST-*ex*clusive amount (which forms part of your income or expenses) when you are only given a GST-*in*clusive amount, divide that amount by 11 to get the GST figure, then deduct from the *in*clusive amount.

| | | |
|---|---|---|
| GST-*in*clusive amount | 440.00 | Total paid out or received by the business |
| *Less* 440.00 divided by 11 | – 40.00 | Amount in GST account |
| = GST-*ex*clusive amount | 400.00 | Amount in income or expense account |

## Test yourself

1.  If the total of your electricity bill is $250.00, what is the GST-exclusive amount?

2.  If you sell goods and issue an invoice totalling $300.00, how much is the GST component?

3.  If $240.00 was posted to an expense account from a supplier invoice, how much did you write the cheque for?

## Answers

| | Calculation | Answer |
|---|---|---|
| 1. | 250/11 = $22.73 GST<br>250 – 22.73 = $227.27 | $227.27 GST exclusive |
| 2. | 300/11 = $27.27 | $27.27 GST |
| 3. | 240 × 10% = $24.00 GST<br>240 + 24 = $264.00 | $264.00 amount of cheque |

# CHAPTER 2
# Marvellous Mobile Phones

Marvellous Mobile Phones (MMP) is a small shop situated in Woodton Shopping Centre. It is owned and run by sole proprietor Adam Wang. The shop specialises in Vodingwell mobile phones which it sells to the public as well as to a few credit customers.

Adam set up the store 3 years ago, using $25,000 of savings and a bank loan of $20,000. The store is open Monday to Saturday. Trish Cornwell is employed to work with Adam during the busy afternoon and Saturday trading periods.

Adam is struggling to keep up with the paperwork and has employed you to take over the manual account-keeping system.

The details of the operation of MMP is summarised in the following paragraphs.

## Sales

Sales to the public are put through the till. Adam banks cash every Monday morning for the preceding week's takings. The deposit is entered into the Cash Receipts Journal *using the previous Saturday's date*.

Adam provides credit to the following customers:

- Ableton University: The University provides mobile phones to its academics and senior management. The phones are sold at a reduced price due to the volume of sales to this organisation. The credit terms are 2/14, n30 which means that Ableton University can obtain an extra 2% early payment discount if they pay within 14 days of the invoice date. If they miss the discount date, they have 30 days in which to pay for the items.

- Magic Mop Cleaning: This is the largest cleaning company in Western Australia. It provides mobile phones to their large workforce, but the cleaners must pay for the phone calls made. Credit terms are 14 days net.

- Mia Mio NL: Mia Mio is a large mining company that provides mobile phones to senior management and certain travelling employees. Again, the phones are sold at a reduced price due to the volume of sales to this organisation. The credit terms are 2/14, net 30.

- Mobilelot Ableton University: Yan Liu, an enterprising student at Ableton University, has set up a booth at the campus, offering mobile phones and accessories to the students. She pays a reduced price and replenishes her stock of phones and accessories every fortnight. Her credit terms are 14 days net.

- Mobilelot Woodton TAFE: Yan's mobile booth at Ableton University was so successful that she helped her friend Wenyi Chan set up a similar booth at the Woodton TAFE. Wenyi also pays a reduced price, replenishes his stock every fortnight and his credit terms are 14 days net.

## Purchases

MMP purchases its inventory items on credit. Adam takes advantage of any discounts offered. All creditors are paid by cheque.

# Goods and Services Tax (GST)

MMP has an Australian Business Number (ABN) of 12 378 945 213 and is registered for GST. The company pays BAS on a monthly basis as Adam likes to pay his liabilities promptly.

MMP charges GST on sales, which is credited to the GST Collected liability account. Remember, GST Collected is not income for MMP as they collect it on behalf of the Australian Taxation Office. MMP can claim back the GST it has paid on business expenses. This is debited to the asset account GST Paid.

When recording the payment of GST and PAYG Withholding liabilities in the Cash Payments Journal, remember that the GST Paid offsets the amounts owed and should be recorded as a negative. This is because a negative debit is a credit.

# Inventory

MMP services a niche market and thus only carries a few inventory items. MMP uses a perpetual inventory system which is recorded on inventory cards. MMP accounts for inventory using the FIFO method: First In, First Out. This means that when recording the Cost of Goods Sold, the first items into inventory are the first sold.

The individual inventory cards that MMP use are as follows:

- Vodingwell 727 mobile phones. These are the top-of-the-line phones with superior functionalities and extra features.
- Vodingwell 443. These are a more basic phone and are priced accordingly. They do not support the internet and are slower than the 727 model.
- Phone covers. As the Vodingwell 727 and 443 are similar in size, the phone covers can be used to protect either phone.
- Phone bling/jewellery. These are little charms or beads that can be attached to the mobile phones to personalise them.
- Hands-free kit. These kits can be used in the car so the customer can talk on the mobile phone without holding the phone.
- Car charger. These chargers are used by the customer to recharge their mobile phone from the cigarette lighter in the car.

A stocktake is performed at the end of every month and adjustments put to a Cost of Goods Sold account called Stock Adjustment.

# Cost of goods sold

As mentioned in the previous section, Cost of Goods Sold is calculated using the FIFO method. Make sure you have a good understanding of this method as using the wrong cost will affect your Cost of Goods Sold account and thus the Income Statement and Trial Balance.

# Wages and PAYG Tax Withholding

MMP pays wages fortnightly to Adam and Trish. PAYG Tax is withheld from the gross wages as per schedules provided by the Australian Tax Office (ATO). Adam will email you the details of gross wages and PAYG tax withheld.

Payment of wages is recorded in the Cash Payments Journal. Note that the column for PAYG tax is a current liability in the Balance Sheet. It is remitted to the ATO monthly with the GST.

On 31 August X1, wages of $1,566.67 was accrued to account 2-150 Accrued Wages.

# Account-keeping policies and procedures

Table 2.1 shows the account-keeping policies and procedures for MMP, including a summary of the important points already mentioned.

| Area | Policies and procedures |
|---|---|
| Sales | • At the end of the month, the till report is printed for the part of the week that finishes that month and is recorded in the Cash Receipts Journal. The last day of the previous month is a Thursday, so the till report was printed and recorded in that month. The money was also deposited on that Thursday. The first till report for October is two days: Friday and Saturday.<br>• Shop takings during the month are banked intact every Monday and recorded in the Cash Receipts Journal *using the ending Saturday's date*.<br>• Receipts for credit customers are banked on the day they are received.<br>• The GST component of the Sales Discount is recorded as a *negative* in the GST Collected column of the Cash Receipts Journal. |
| Purchases | • Credit suppliers are paid in sufficient time to receive early payment discounts, when offered by the supplier.<br>• The GST component of the Purchase Discount is recorded as a *negative* in the GST Paid column of the Cash Payments Journal. |
| Inventory and Cost of Goods Sold | • Inventory cards are updated with every sale or purchase.<br>• Cost of Goods Sold is calculated using the FIFO method and recorded in the relevant journal with every sale. |
| Stocktake | • Stocktake is performed monthly with inventory adjustments going to the Stock Adjustment account. |
| Wages | • Wages are paid by EFT fortnightly on a Wednesday. The pay period is Wednesday to Tuesday. |
| Prepayments | • Radio advertising for September and October was purchased on 30 August 20X1 for $550.00 (GST inclusive). It was recorded in the Prepaid Advertising Account.<br>• A 12-month insurance policy of $1790.00 (including GST of $110.00) was paid on 1 December 20X0. It was recorded in the Prepaid Insurance account. |
| Depreciation | • Office Equipment is depreciated at 30% p.a. using diminishing value method.<br>• Shop furniture/fixtures is depreciated at 15% p.a. using straight-line method. |
| Petty Cash | • A petty cash imprest system is used to buy small items. The float is $200.00.<br>• Petty cash vouchers must be filled out with every petty cash purchase. |
| Loan | • The $20,000.00 loan is interest-only at 6% p.a. The interest is direct-debited from the cheque account on the last working day of every month. The loan is due to be repaid on 12 March 20X2. |
| Bank Reconciliation | • The cheque account ledger is reconciled with the bank statement at the end of the month.<br>• There may be transactions present in the bank statement that are not present in the cash journals. These need to be journalised and posted to the appropriate special journal before the financial statements are prepared. |
| End-of-Month Journals | • A checklist is provided at the end of the source documents. |

*Table 2.1    MMP's account-keeping policies and procedures*

# CHAPTER 3
# Manual account-keeping information

Table 3.1 shows the ledgers, journals and schedules used in maintaining the manual accounting records for Marvellous Mobile Phones.

| Title | Purpose |
|---|---|
| Sales Journal | Records all credit sales |
| Purchases Journal | Records all inventory credit purchases |
| Cash Receipts Journal | Records all cash receipts from shop sales and debtors |
| Cash Payments Journal | Records all payments to creditors and sundry purchases |
| General Journal | Records all transactions that can't be recorded in the above journals such as non-inventory credit sales and purchases, sales and purchase returns and adjusting and closing journals |
| Subsidiary Ledgers | Records a running balance for the individual debtor (accounts receivable) and creditor (accounts payable) |
| Schedules | Provides a "snap shot" of what makes up the balance in the control accounts: accounts receivable, accounts payable and inventory |
| Inventory Cards | Records a running balance of the flow of inventory in and out as sales and purchases are made. |

*Table 3.1      Ledgers, journals and schedules used for Marvellous Mobile Phones manual account-keeping system*

# Instructions

Tick each instruction once you have completed it.

- Review the preceding chapter to gain familiarity with the business.

- Enter the opening balances from the Trial Balance (Figure 3.2) into the General Ledger accounts in chapter 5.

- Enter the balances owing for 1st September from the Accounts Receivable Schedule (Figure 3.3) into the Accounts Receivable Subsidiary Ledger in chapter 7.

- Enter the balances owed from the Accounts Payable Schedule (Figure 3.4) into the Accounts Payable Subsidiary Ledger in chapter 7.

- Compare the Inventory Schedule (Figure 3.5) with the Inventory cards, which already have the opening balances.

- On the first of September 20X1, make the reversing entry for accrued wages ($1,566.67).

- Using the source documents in chapter 4, record and post all transactions in accordance with the account-keeping policies and procedures in the previous chapter. *Remember to calculate Cost of Goods Sold using the FIFO method.*

- Prepare a bank reconciliation, using the Cash Receipts Journal and Cash Payments Journal in chapter 5 and the Bank Statement at the end of chapter 4. Record any transactions present in the bank statement (but not the journals) into the appropriate special journal.

- Complete and post all end-of-month journals according to the procedures in chapter 2. A check list of these adjustments is provided at the end of chapter 4.

- Prepare the Accounts Receivable, Accounts Payable and Inventory schedule as at the end of September 20X1. Ensure these reconcile with the appropriate control accounts.
- Using the worksheet, prepare an unadjusted Trial Balance as at 30 September 20X1. Record the balance day adjustments in the worksheet and complete the rest of the worksheet.
- Record the balance day adjustments in the general journal and post to the general ledger.
- Complete the income statement and balance sheet provided. Note the dates.
- Prepare and post closing general journal entries.
- Prepare the post-closing trial balance.

Note: Businesses don't actually close off their general ledger accounts at the end of every month to produce their financial statements. We adjust and close off the accounts in this practice set to give you experience in the complete accounting cycle.

Hint: Every special journal must balance before being entered into the General Ledger accounts. Remember the universal rule for double-entry accounting: the sum of the debits must equal the sum of the credits. The exception, of course, is the Cost of Goods Sold columns, which are balanced by the same amount being posted to Merchandise Inventory.

**Marvellous Mobile Phones**
**Chart of Accounts**

| *Account number* | *Account name* | *Account number* | *Account name* |
|---|---|---|---|
| | **Current Assets** | | **Income** |
| 1-101 | Cheque Account PSI 7467 | 4-101 | Sales – Mobile Phones |
| 1-102 | Investment Account | 4-201 | Sales – Accessories |
| 1-120 | Petty Cash | 4-701 | Sales Discounts |
| 1-201 | Accounts Receivable | 4-801 | Sales Returns |
| 1-202 | Allowance Doubtful Debts | 4-901 | Interest Received |
| 1-300 | Merchandise Inventory | | **Cost of Goods Sold** |
| 1-400 | GST Paid | 5-101 | COGS Mobile Phones |
| 1-500 | Prepaid Insurance | 5-201 | COGS Accessories |
| 1-510 | Prepaid Advertising | 5-701 | Purchase Discount/Return |
| | **Non-Current Assets** | 5-910 | Freight Paid |
| 1-701 | Office Equip. at Cost | 5-920 | Stock Adjustments |
| 1-702 | Office Equip. Accum. Dep'n | | **Expense** |
| 1-801 | Shop Furn./Fixtures at Cost | 6-101 | Advertising Expense |
| 1-802 | Shop Furn./Fix. Accum. Dep'n | 6-102 | Accounting/Legal |
| | **Current Liabilities** | 6-103 | Bank Charges |
| 2-120 | Accounts Payable | 6-111 | Depreciation Expense |
| 2-131 | GST Collected | 6-211 | Electricity |
| 2-141 | Superannuation Payable | 6-212 | Insurance |
| 2-142 | PAYG Withholding Payable | 6-213 | Donations |
| 2-150 | Accrued Wages | 6-214 | Rent |
| | **Non-Current Liabilities** | 6-215 | Stationery/Printing |
| 2-210 | Bank Loan | 6-216 | Telephone/Internet |
| | **Equity** | 6-217 | Postage |
| 3-101 | Owner Equity – Adam | 6-301 | Wages Expense |
| 3-102 | Owner Drawings – Adam | 6-302 | Superannuation Expense |
| 3-200 | Income Summary | 6-303 | Staff Amenities |
| | | 6-901 | Interest Expense |
| | | 6-902 | Bad/Doubt. Debt Expense |

*Figure 3.1*      *Chart of Accounts*

**Marvellous Mobile Phones**

**Post-Closing Trial Balance**

**As at 31 August 20X1**

|  |  | DR | CR |
|---|---|---|---|
| 1-101 | Cheque Account PSI 7467 | 7,119.51 | |
| 1-102 | Investment Account | 10,326.67 | |
| 1-120 | Petty Cash | 200.00 | |
| 1-201 | Accounts Receivable | 7,390.90 | |
| 1-202 | Allowance Doubtful Debts | | 147.82 |
| 1-300 | Merchandise Inventory | 14,675.50 | |
| 1-400 | GST Paid | 1,156.00 | |
| 1-500 | Prepaid Insurance | 420.00 | |
| 1-510 | Prepaid Advertising | 500.00 | |
| 1-701 | Office Equipment at Cost | 6,470.00 | |
| 1-702 | Office Equipment Accum. Dep'n | | 1,050.78 |
| 1-801 | Shop Furn./Fixtures at Cost | 9,200.00 | |
| 1-802 | Shop Furn./Fix. Accum. Dep. | | 690.00 |
| 2-120 | Accounts Payable | | 273.31 |
| 2-131 | GST Collected | | 3,776.00 |
| 2-141 | Superannuation Payable | | 414.00 |
| 2-142 | PAYG Withholding Payable | | 700.00 |
| 2-150 | Accrued Wages | | 1,566.67 |
| 2-210 | Bank Loans | | 20,000.00 |
| 3-101 | Owner Equity – Adam | | 25,000.00 |
| 3-102 | Owner Drawing – Adam | 4,000.00 | |
| 3-200 | Income Summary | | 7,840.00 |
|  | TOTALS | 61,458.58 | 61,458.58 |

Figure 3.2    Post-closing trial balance as at 31 August 20X1

**Accounts Receivable**
**As at 31 August 20X1**

| Code | Customer | Invoice date | Invoice no. | Amount |
|------|----------|--------------|-------------|--------|
| ABE01 | Ableton University | 30/08/X1 | 893 | 4851.00 |
| MAG01 | Magic Mop Cleaning | 17/08/X1 | 890 | 1945.90 |
| MOB01 | Mobilelot – Ableton Uni | 23/08/X1 | 891 | 303.60 |
| MOB02 | Mobilelot – Woodton TAFE | 28/08/X1 | 892 | 290.40 |
| 1-201 | Accounts Receivable Control | | | 7390.90 |

*Figure 3.3*        *Schedule of Accounts Receivable*

**Accounts Payable**
**As at 31 August 20X1**

| Code | Supplier | Invoice date | Invoice no. | Amount |
|------|----------|--------------|-------------|--------|
| TEL01 | Telpho Communications | 25/08/X1 | 754 228 104 | 222.31 |
| FON01 | Fone Bling | 23/08/X1 | A43 | 51.00 |
| 2-120 | Accounts Payable Control | | | 273.31 |

*Figure 3.4*        *Schedule of Accounts Payable*

**Inventory Schedule**
**As at 31 August 20X1**

| Code | Description | Qty | Amount |
|------|-------------|-----|--------|
| BLI01 | Bling/jewellery | 149 | 223.50 |
| CAR01 | Car charger | 16 | 224.00 |
| COV01 | Phone covers | 26 | 338.00 |
| HAN01 | Hands-free Kit | 10 | 350.00 |
| V-727 | Vodingwell 727 | 22 | 12,760.00 |
| V-443 | Vodingwell 443 | 6 | 780.00 |
| 1-300 | Inventory Control | | 14,675.50 |

*Figure 3.5*        *Schedule of Inventory*

# CHAPTER 4
# Source documents

## Transactions for Friday 1 to Saturday 2 September 20X1

**Woodton Shopping Centre**
ABN 32 008 684 740

24 Woodton Ave
Woodton WA 6008

Ph: 9381 5569
Fax: 9381 9351

### TAX INVOICE

Marvellous Mobile Phones
PO BOX 8022
WOODTON WA 6008

Invoice MMPSept.X1
Dated 01/09/X1

PREMISES:
Shop 6A
Woodton Shopping Centre

| | |
|---|---|
| Rent for September 20X1 | $600.00 |
| GST | $60.00 |
| **Due 1 September X1** | **$660.00** |

---

### Petty cash voucher

Date: 1/9/X1   Voucher: 642

Amount: $13.20

Description: Australia Post stamps

| Account | Amount | GST |
|---|---|---|
| Postage | $12.00 | $1.20 |
| | | |

Signature: T. Cornwell

### Petty cash voucher

Date: 2/9/X1   Voucher: 643

Amount: $2.40

Description: Doolies Milk

| Account | Amount | GST |
|---|---|---|
| Staff Amens | $2.40 | 0.00 |
| | | |

Signature: T. Cornwell

## Transactions for Monday 4 to Saturday 9 September 20X1

| Till report Marvellous Mobile Phones Friday 1 to Saturday 2 September 20X1 | | | | | | |
|---|---|---|---|---|---|---|
| | | | | | Number T1703 | |
| Sales account | Code | Description | Qty | Sales price ex-GST | Total ex-GST | Tax code |
| 4-201 | BLI01 | Bling/jewellery | 8 | 3.00 | 24.00 | GST |
| 4-201 | COV01 | Phone covers | 2 | 25.00 | 50.00 | GST |
| 4-201 | HAN01 | Hands-free kit | 4 | 70.00 | 280.00 | GST |
| 4-101 | V-443 | Vodingwell 443 phone | 2 | 260.00 | 520.00 | GST |
| | | | | Subtotal | 874.00 | |
| | | | | GST | 87.40 | |
| | Banked 04/09/x1 | | | Total | 961.40 | |

---

**Deposit receipt**          Ψ PSI BANK

**Date:** *2 Sept. 20X1*
**Branch:** *Woodton*
**Account name:** *Marvellous Mobile Phones*
**Account no.:** *3423 7467*
**Details:** *Till receipts (T1703)*
**Amount:** *$961.40*

Teller
MB

---

**Deposit receipt**          Ψ PSI BANK

**Date:** *7 Sept. 20X1*
**Branch:** *Woodton*
**Account name:** *Marvellous Mobile Phones*
**Account no.:** *3423 7467*
**Details:** *Mobilelot Ableton Uni (inv 891)*
**Amount:** *$303.60*

Teller
LK

---

### Petty cash voucher

Date: 4/9/X1   Voucher: 644

Amount: $16.50
Description: Lou Elens Bakery Birthday Cake

| Account | Amount | GST |
|---|---|---|
| Staff Amens | $15.00 | $1.50 |
| | | |

Signature: A. Wang

---

### Petty cash voucher

Date: 7/9/X1   Voucher: 645

Amount: $4.80
Description: Doolies Milk

| Account | Amount | GST |
|---|---|---|
| Staff Amens | $4.80 | 0.00 |
| | | |

Signature: T. Cornwell

## *Marvellous Mobile Phones*

## Purchase order
ABN 12 378 945 213

Shop 6A
Woodton Shopping Centre
24 Woodton Ave
Woodton WA 6008
Ph: 9312 4664 Fax: 9312 4676

| SUPPLIER | Vodingwell | Date: | 4 Sept. 20X1 |
| | 12 Paper Street, | PO no.: | P1232 |
| | Melbourne VIC 3147 | | |

| Qty | Description | Unit price | Ex-GST |
|---|---|---|---|
| 5 | Vodingwell 727 | 580.00 | 2900.00 |
| 7 | Vodingwell 443 | 130.00 | 910.00 |
| | | SUBTOTAL | 3810.00 |
| | | GST | 381.00 |
| | | TOTAL | 4191.00 |

| **Date:** 5 Sept. 20X1 | **Date:** 5 Sept. 20X1 | **Date:** 5 Sept. 20X1 |
|---|---|---|
| **To:** Telpho Corp | **To:** Fone Bling | **To:** Woodton Shopping Centre |
| **For:** Inv 754 228 104 | **For:** Inv A43 | **For:** Inv MMPSeptX1 |
| **Amount:** $222.31 | **Amount:** $51.00 | **Amount:** $660.00 |
| **Cheque 2068** | **Cheque 2069** | **Cheque 2070** |

# Vodingwell
12 Paper St, Melbourne VIC 3147
Ph: (03) 9422 3611 Fax: (03) 9422 3688
ABN 29 058 152 604

| **Tax invoice:** | 76496 | **CUSTOMER** | Marvellous Mobile Phones |
| **PO no.:** | P1232 | | Shop 6A, Woodton Shop Ctr |
| **Date:** | 06/09/X1 | | 24 Woodton Ave |
| | | | Woodton WA 6008 |

| QTY | PRODUCT CODE | DESCRIPTION | UNIT PRICE | LINE TOTAL EX-GST |
|---|---|---|---|---|
| 5 | V14727 | Vodingwell 727 | 580.00 | $2900.00 |
| 7 | V23443 | Vodingwell 443 | 130.00 | $910.00 |
| | | | SUBTOTAL | $3810.00 |
| **TERMS:** | 5% 14 net 30 | | GST | $381.00 |
| **SHIP:** | Express | | TOTAL | $4191.00 |

## Accounts

| | |
|---|---|
| **From:** | Adam Wang |
| **Sent:** | 6 September 20X1 |
| **To:** | Accounts |
| **Subject:** | Please process pays today, pay period 22 August to 5 September 20X1 |

Hi

I have paid wages today by EFT from the cheque account. Please record the following wages into the Cash Payments Journal.

| | *Adam* | *Trish* |
|---|---|---|
| Gross | $1800.00 | $500.00 |
| Tax | −$320.00 | −$30.00 |
| Net wages | $1480.00 | $470.00 |

Thanks, Adam

---

### Marvellous Mobile Phones

Shop 6A, Woodton Shopping Centre
24 Woodton Ave
Woodton WA 6008
Ph: 9312 4664 Fax: 9312 4676

**Tax invoice**
ABN 12 378 945 213

CUSTOMER  Yan Liu
Mobilelot Ableton
Ph: 0404 288 111

Date: 7 Sept. 20X1
Invoice no.: 894
Terms: 14 days

| Qty | Description | Unit price | Ex-GST |
|---|---|---|---|
| 7 | COV01 Phone covers | 20.00 | 140.00 |
| 14 | BLI01  Bling/jewellery | 2.00 | 28.00 |
| 4 | V-443  Vodingwell 443 phones | 200.00 | 800.00 |
| | | SUBTOTAL | 968.00 |
| | | GST | 96.80 |
| | | TOTAL | 1064.80 |

Marvellous Mobiles
BSB: 016-499
Account: 3423 7467

---

**Phone Bits**
81 Gympie Way, Willetton WA 6155
Ph: 9372 6666

ABN 24 129 809 749

**TO:** Marvellous Mobile Phones
PO Box 8022
Woodton WA 6008

**TAX INVOICE:** 6321
**DATE:** 8/9/X1

| QTY | DESCRIPTION | COST | AMOUNT | TAX |
|---|---|---|---|---|
| 3 | Hands-free kit | 35.00 | 105.00 | GST |
| 9 | Phone covers for Vodingwells 443/727 | 13.00 | 117.00 | GST |
| | Freight | 7.00 | 7.00 | GST |
| | | Subtotal | 229.00 | |
| | | GST | 22.90 | |
| **Terms** 14 days | | Total | 251.90 | |

**THE ELECTRICITY CO. – TAX INVOICE**
ABN: 71 743 446 839

Enquiries: 13 13 13
Payable: 23 Sept. X1
Invoice no.: 734 718 56

Account Number
**25 778 0473**

Date of issue
8/09/20X1

Marvellous Mobile Phones
PO Box 8022, Woodton WA 6008

GPO Box U113
Perth WA 6845

| | | |
|---|---|---|
| Current charges: | $465.52 | |
| + previous charges | + $426.69 | |
| – previous payment | – $426.69 | |
| Balance: | $465.52 | |

(Includes GST of $42.32)

---

*Marvellous Mobile Phones*

Shop 6A, Woodton Shopping Centre
24 Woodton Ave
Woodton WA 6008
Ph: 9312 4664 Fax: 9312 4676

**Tax invoice**
ABN 12 378 945 213

CUSTOMER    Mia Mio NL
32 Outram Street
West Perth WA 6000

Date:    8 Sept. 20X1
Invoice no.:    895
Terms:    2/14 Net 30

| Qty | Description | Unit price | Ex-GST |
|---|---|---|---|
| 10 | V-727  Vodingwell 727 phones | 828.00 | 8280.00 |
| 10 | COV01 Phone covers | 22.50 | 225.00 |
| 10 | CAR01 Car charger | 31.50 | 315.00 |
| | | SUBTOTAL | 8820.00 |
| | | GST | 882.00 |
| | | TOTAL | 9702.00 |

Marvellous Mobiles
BSB: 016-499
Account: 3423 7467

## Transactions for Monday 11 to Saturday 16 September 20X1

| Petty cash voucher |
|---|

Date: 11/9/X1   Voucher: 646

Amount: $3.85
Description: Doolies
Biscuits

| Account | Amount | GST |
|---|---|---|
| Staff Amens | $3.50 | $0.35 |
| | | |

Signature: A. Wang

| Petty cash voucher |
|---|

Date: 14/9/X1   Voucher: 647

Amount: $42.35
Description: Stationery Plus
Pens, paper

| Account | Amount | GST |
|---|---|---|
| Stationery | $38.50 | 3.85 |
| | | |

Signature: T. Cornwell

### Till report
### Marvellous Mobile Phones
### Monday 4 to Saturday 9 September 20X1

Number T1704

| Sales account | Code | Description | Qty | Sales price ex-GST | Total ex-GST | Tax code |
|---|---|---|---|---|---|---|
| 4-201 | BLI01 | Bling/jewellery | 4 | 3.00 | 12.00 | GST |
| 4-201 | CAR01 | Car charger | 2 | 35.00 | 70.00 | GST |
| 4-201 | COV01 | Phone covers | 8 | 25.00 | 200.00 | GST |
| 4-201 | HAN01 | Hands-free kit | 4 | 70.00 | 280.00 | GST |
| 4-101 | V-727 | Vodingwell 727 phone | 1 | 920.00 | 920.00 | GST |
| 4-101 | V-443 | Vodingwell 443 phone | 1 | 260.00 | 260.00 | GST |
| | | | | Subtotal | 1742.00 | |
| | | | | GST | 174.20 | |
| | | Banked *11/09/X1* | | Total | 1916.20 | |

---

## Deposit receipt                    Ψ PSI BANK

**Date:** *09 Sept. 20X1*
**Branch:** *Woodton*
**Account name:** *Marvellous Mobile Phones*
**Account no.:** *3423 7467*
**Details:** *Till receipts (T1704)*
**Amount:** *$1916.20*

Teller
FM

---

## Deposit receipt                    Ψ PSI BANK

**Date:** *11 Sept. 20X1*
**Branch:** *Woodton*
**Account name:** *Marvellous Mobile Phones*
**Account no.:** *3423 7467*
**Details:** *Mobilelot Woodton TAFE (inv 892)*
**Amount:** *$290.40*

Teller
LK

---

## *Marvellous Mobile Phones*

Shop 6A, Woodton Shopping Centre
24 Woodton Ave
Woodton WA 6008
Ph: 9312 4664 Fax: 9312 4676

### Credit Note
ABN 12 378 945 213

CUSTOMER    Yan Liu
            Mobilelot Ableton
            Ph: 0404 288 111

Date:       11 Sept. X1
Credit no.:   Cr41

| Qty | Description | Unit price | Ex-GST |
|---|---|---|---|
| −2 | COV01 Phone covers (stitching came undone) | 20.00 | −40.00 |
| | SUBTOTAL | | −40.00 |
| | GST | | −4.00 |
| | TOTAL | | −44.00 |

Marvellous Mobiles
BSB: 016-499
Account: 3423 7467

## Marvellous Mobile Phones — Tax Invoice

**Marvellous Mobile Phones**
Shop 6A, Woodton Shopping Centre
24 Woodton Ave
Woodton WA 6008
Ph: 9312 4664 Fax: 9312 4676

**Tax Invoice**
ABN 12 378 945 213

| CUSTOMER | Wenyi Chan | | |
|---|---|---|---|
| | Mobilelot Woodton | Date: | 11 Sept. X1 |
| | Ph: 0414 314 272 | Invoice no.: | 896 |
| | | Terms: | 14 days |

| Qty | Description | Unit price | Ex-GST |
|---|---|---|---|
| 2 | COV01 Phone covers | 20.00 | 40.00 |
| 10 | BLI01  Bling/jewellery | 2.00 | 20.00 |
| 2 | V-443   Vodingwell 443 | 200.00 | 400.00 |
| | | SUBTOTAL | 460.00 |
| | | GST | 46.00 |
| | | TOTAL | 506.00 |

Marvellous Mobiles
BSB: 016-499
Account: 3423 7467

## Marvellous Mobile Phones — Purchase Order

**Marvellous Mobile Phones**
Shop 6A, Woodton Shopping Centre
24 Woodton Ave
Woodton WA 6008
Ph: 9312 4664 Fax: 9312 4676

**Purchase Order**
ABN 12 378 945 213

| CUSTOMER | Vodingwell | | |
|---|---|---|---|
| | 12 Paper Street, | Date: | 13 Sept. X1 |
| | Melbourne VIC 3147 | PO no.: | P1233 |

| Qty | Description | Unit price | Ex-GST |
|---|---|---|---|
| 4 | Vodingwell 727 | 580.00 | 2320.00 |
| 5 | Vodingwell 443 | 130.00 | 650.00 |
| | | SUBTOTAL | 2970.00 |
| | | GST | 297.00 |
| | | TOTAL | 3267.00 |

Marvellous Mobiles
BSB: 016-499
Account: 3423 7467

## Phone Bits — Credit Note

**Phone Bits**
81 Gympie Way, Willetton WA 6155
Ph: 9372 6666

TO: Marvellous Mobile Phones
PO Box 8022
Woodton WA 6008

ABN 24 129 809 749

**CREDIT NOTE:** 21
**DATE:** 14/9/X1

| QTY | DESCRIPTION | COST | AMOUNT | TAX |
|---|---|---|---|---|
| −2 | Phone covers for Vodingwells 443/727 | 13.00 | −26.00 | GST |
| | Subtotal | | −26.00 | |
| | GST | | −2.60 | |
| | Total | | −28.60 | |

| Deposit receipt | Ψ PSI BANK |
|---|---|

**Date:** *13 Sept. 20X1*
**Branch:** *Woodton*
**Account name:** *Marvellous Mobile Phones*
**Account no.:** *3423 7467*
**Details:** *Ableton University (inv 893) less discount*
**Amount:** *$4753.98*

| Teller |
|---|
| AM |

| Deposit receipt | Ψ PSI BANK |
|---|---|

**Date:** *14 Sept. 20X1*
**Branch:** *Woodton*
**Account name:** *Marvellous Mobile Phones*
**Account no.:** *3423 7467*
**Details:** *Magic Mop (inv 890)*
**Amount:** *$1945.90*

| Teller |
|---|
| VK |

# Vodingwell

12 Paper St, Melbourne VIC 3147
Ph: (03) 9422 3611 Fax: (03) 9422 3688
ABN 29 058 152 604

| Tax invoice: | 77132 | **CUSTOMER** | Marvellous Mobile Phones |
|---|---|---|---|
| PO no.: | P1233 | | Shop 6A, Woodton Shop Ctr |
| Date: | 15/09/X1 | | 24 Woodton Ave |
| | | | Woodton WA 6008 |

| QTY | PRODUCT CODE | DESCRIPTION | UNIT PRICE | LINE TOTAL EX-GST |
|---|---|---|---|---|
| 4 | V14727 | Vodingwell 727 | 580.00 | $2320.00 |
| 5 | V23443 | Vodingwell 443 | 130.00 | $650.00 |
| | | | SUBTOTAL | $2970.00 |
| **TERMS:** | 5% 14 net 30 | | GST | $297.00 |
| **SHIP:** | Express | | TOTAL | $3267.00 |

| *Phone Bits* | | **TO:** | Marvellous Mobile Phones |
|---|---|---|---|
| 81 Gympie Way, Willetton WA 6155 | | | PO Box 8022 |
| Ph: 9372 6666 | | | Woodton WA 6008 |
| | | **TAX INVOICE:** 6471 | |
| ABN 24 129 809 749 | | **DATE:** 15/9/X1 | |

| QTY | DESCRIPTION | COST | AMOUNT | TAX |
|---|---|---|---|---|
| 16 | Car charger | 16.00 | 256.00 | GST |
| 12 | Hands-free kit | 37.00 | 444.00 | GST |
| 9 | Phone covers for Vodingwells 443/727 | 15.00 | 135.00 | GST |
| | Freight | 9.00 | 9.00 | |
| | | Subtotal | 844.00 | |
| | | GST | 84.40 | |
| **Terms:** | 14 days | Total | 928.40 | |

# Transactions for Monday 18 to Saturday 23 September 20X1

| Till report<br>Marvellous Mobile Phones<br>Monday 11 to Saturday 16 September 20X1 | | | | | | |
|---|---|---|---|---|---|---|
| | | | | | Number T1705 | |
| Sales account | Code | Description | Qty | Sales price ex-GST | Total ex-GST | Tax code |
| 4-201 | BLI01 | Bling/jewellery | 9 | 3.00 | 27.00 | GST |
| 4-201 | COV01 | Phone covers | 3 | 25.00 | 75.00 | GST |
| 4-201 | HAN01 | Hands-free kit | 2 | 70.00 | 140.00 | GST |
| 4-101 | V-727 | Vodingwell 727 phone | 2 | 920.00 | 1840.00 | GST |
| | | | | Subtotal | 2082.00 | |
| | | | | GST | 208.20 | |
| Banked 18/09/x1 | | | | Total | 2290.20 | |

---

**Deposit receipt**　　Ψ　PSI BANK

**Date:** *16 Sept. 20X1*
**Branch:** *Woodton*
**Account name:** *Marvellous Mobile Phones*
**Account no.:** *3423 7467*
**Details:** *Till receipts (T1705)*
**Amount: $2290.20**

| Teller |
|---|
| MF |

---

**Deposit receipt**　　Ψ　PSI BANK

**Date:** *20 Sept. 20X1*
**Branch:** *Woodton*
**Account name:** *Marvellous Mobile Phones*
**Account no.:** *3423 7467*
**Details:** *Mia Mio NL (inv 895) including discount*
**Amount: $9507.96**

| Teller |
|---|
| VC |

---

## Petty cash voucher

Date: 18/9/x1　Voucher: 648

Amount: $4.80

Description: Doolies
Milk

| Account | Amount | GST |
|---|---|---|
| Staff amens | $4.80 | 0.00 |
| | | |

Signature: A. Wang

---

## Petty cash voucher

Date: 22/9/x1　Voucher: 649

Amount: $50.00

Description: Cat Haven
Donation

| Account | Amount | GST |
|---|---|---|
| Donations | $50.00 | 0.00 |
| | | |

Signature: A. Wang

*Marvellous Mobile Phones*

Shop 6A, Woodton Shopping Centre
24 Woodton Ave
Woodton WA 6008
Ph: 9312 4664 Fax: 9312 4676

**Tax Invoice**
ABN 12 378 945 213

| CUSTOMER | Ableton University | | | Date: | 20 Sept. X1 |
| | Kent Street | | | Invoice no.: | 897 |
| | Ableton WA 6147 | | | Terms: | 2/14 n30 |

| Qty | Description | Unit price | Ex-GST |
|---|---|---|---|
| 4 | Vodingwell 727 | 828.00 | 3312.00 |
| | | | 3312.00 |

Marvellous Mobiles
BSB: 016-499
Account: 3423 7467

| | |
|---|---|
| | 3312.00 |
| GST | 331.20 |
| TOTAL | 3643.20 |

---

*Marvellous Mobile Phones*

Shop 6A, Woodton Shopping Centre
24 Woodton Ave
Woodton WA 6008
Ph: 9312 4664 Fax: 9312 4676

**Tax Invoice**
ABN 12 378 945 213

| CUSTOMER | Yan Liu | | | Date: | 21 Sept. X1 |
| | Mobilelot Ableton | | | Invoice no.: | 898 |
| | Ph: 0404 288 111 | | | Terms: | 14 days |

| Qty | Description | Unit price | Ex-GST |
|---|---|---|---|
| 3 | V-727  Vodingwell 727 | 850.00 | 2550.00 |
| 3 | COV01 Phone cover | 22.50 | 67.50 |
| 4 | CAR01 Car charger | 31.50 | 126.00 |
| | SUBTOTAL | | 2743.50 |

Marvellous Mobiles
BSB: 016-499
Account: 3423 7467

| | |
|---|---|
| SUBTOTAL | 2743.50 |
| GST | 274.35 |
| TOTAL | 3017.85 |

---

| **Date:** 18 Sept. 20X1 | **Date:** 19 Sept. 20X1 | **Date:** 19 Sept. 20X1 |
|---|---|---|
| **To:** Vodingwell | **To:** Phone Bits | **To:** Electricity Co. |
| **For:** Inv 79496 | **For:** Inv 6321 | **For:** Inv 734 718 56 |
| less discount | less credit | |
| **Amount:** $3981.45 | **Amount:** $223.30 | **Amount:** $465.52 |
| **Cheque 2071** | **Cheque 2072** | **Cheque 2073** |

## Accounts

| | |
|---|---|
| **From:** | Adam Wang |
| **Sent:** | 20 September 20X1 |
| **To:** | Accounts |
| **Subject:** | Please process pays today, pay period 6 September to 19 September 20X1 |

Hi

I have paid wages today by EFT from the cheque account. Please record the following wages into the Cash Payments Journal.

| | *Adam* | *Trish* |
|---|---|---|
| Gross | $1800.00 | $500.00 |
| Tax | −$320.00 | −$30.00 |
| Net wages | $1480.00 | $470.00 |

Thanks, Adam

---

| Deposit receipt | Ψ PSI BANK |
|---|---|

**Date:** *21 Sept. 20X1*
**Branch:** *Woodton*
**Account name:** *Marvellous Mobile Phones*
**Account no.:** *3423 7467*
**Details:** *Mobilot Ableton (inv 894) less credit*
**Amount:** *$1020.80*

| Teller |
|---|
| MF |

## Transactions for Monday 25 to Saturday 30 September 20X1

*T*elpho
ABN 33 051 775 556

**Tax invoice**
Issued 25/09/X1

Bill enquiries 13 22 00
GPO Box 1901
Melbourne VIC 3001

**Your Bill  768 123 197**

**Total Due: $232.87**
**Pay by: 8 October X1**

Marvellous Mobile Phones
PO Box 8022
Woodton WA 6008

**Your Account Summary**

| | | |
|---|---|---|
| Balance outstanding | 0.00 | Your account: 2000 0914 5004 |
| New charges | $232.87 | Your phone no.: 08 9312 4664 |
| (See over for breakdown) | | Your fax no.: 08 9312 4676 |
| **Total due** | **$232.87** | |
| GST included in new charges | $21.17 | |

| Till report |
|---|
| Marvellous Mobile Phones |
| **Monday 18 to Saturday 23 September 20X1** |

Number T1706

| Sales account | Code | Description | Qty | Sales price ex-GST | Total ex-GST | Tax code |
|---|---|---|---|---|---|---|
| 4-201 | BLI01 | Bling/jewellery | 11 | 3.00 | 33.00 | GST |
| 4-201 | CAR01 | Car charger | 3 | 35.00 | 105.00 | GST |
| 4-201 | COV01 | Phone covers | 4 | 25.00 | 100.00 | GST |
| 4-201 | HAN01 | Hands-free kit | 2 | 70.00 | 140.00 | GST |
| 4-101 | V-727 | Vodingwell 727 phone | 2 | 920.00 | 1840.00 | GST |
| 4-101 | V-443 | Vodingwell 443 phone | 2 | 260.00 | 520.00 | GST |
| | | | | Subtotal | 2738.00 | |
| | | | | GST | 273.80 | |
| Banked 25/09/x1 | | | | Total | 3011.80 | |

**Deposit receipt**          Ψ PSI BANK

**Date:** *23 Sept. 20X1*
**Branch:** *Woodton*
**Account name:** *Marvellous Mobile Phones*
**Account no.:** *3423 7467*
**Details:** *Till Receipts (T1706)*
**Amount:** *$3011.80*

| Teller |
|---|
| MF |

**Deposit receipt**          Ψ PSI BANK

**Date:** *25 Sept. 20X1*
**Branch:** *Woodton*
**Account name:** *Marvellous Mobile Phones*
**Account no.:** *3423 7467*
**Details:** *Mobilot Ableton (inv 896)*
**Amount:** *$506.00*

| Teller |
|---|
| FM |

---

**Date:** 26 Sept. 20x1
**To:** Vodingwell
**For:** Inv 77132 less discount
**Amount:** $3103.65
**Cheque 2074**

**Date:** 26 Sept. 20X1
**To:** TEST Super
**For:** Superannuation for August
**Amount:** $414.00
**Cheque 2075**

**Date:** 28 Sept. 20X1
**To:** Phone Bits
**For:** Inv 6471
**Amount:** $928.40
**Cheque 2076**

---

**Date:** 28 Sept. 20x1
**To:** Stationery Plus
**For:** Stationery
**Amount:** $112.20
**Cheque 2077**

**Date:** 29 Sept. 20X1
**To:** Stationery Plus
**For:** Printer (to be picked up on 1 October)
**Amount:** $880.00
**Cheque 2078**

**Date:** 29 Sept. 20X1
**To:** Cash
**For:** Petty Cash
**Amount:** $137.90
**Cheque 2079**

## Accounts

| | |
|---|---|
| **From:** | Adam Wang |
| **Sent:** | 29 September 20X1 |
| **To:** | Accounts |
| **Subject:** | BPAY to Australian Tax Office for August 20X1 BAS |

Hi

I have paid the ATO $2672.00 by BPAY today for the August 20X1 BAS. The details are:

| | |
|---|---|
| GST Collected | $3104.00 |
| PAYG Withholding | +$ 700.00 |
| *less* GST Paid | −$1132.00 |
| BPAY | $2672.00 |

Thanks, Adam

---

*Marvellous Mobile Phones*

Shop 6A, Woodton Shopping Centre
24 Woodton Ave
Woodton WA 6008
Ph: 9312 4664 Fax: 9312 4676

**Tax invoice**
ABN 12 378 945 213

| | | |
|---|---|---|
| CUSTOMER | Wenyi Chan | |
| | Mobilelot Woodton | |
| | Ph: 0414 314 272 | |

| | |
|---|---|
| Date: | 25 Sept. X1 |
| Invoice no.: | 899 |
| Terms: | 14 days |

| Qty | Description | Unit price | Ex-GST |
|---|---|---|---|
| 4 | CAR01 Car charger | 22.00 | 88.00 |
| 8 | BLI01  Bling/jewellery | 2.00 | 16.00 |
| 1 | V-443  Vodingwell 443 phones | 200.00 | 200.00 |
| | | SUBTOTAL | 304.00 |
| | | GST | 30.40 |
| | | TOTAL | 334.40 |

Marvellous Mobile
BSB: 016-499
Account: 3423 7467

---

Till report
Marvellous Mobile Phones
### Monday 25 to Saturday 30 September 20X1

Number T1707

| Sales account | Code | Description | Qty | Sales price ex-GST | Total ex-GST | Tax code |
|---|---|---|---|---|---|---|
| 4-201 | BLI01 | Bling/jewellery | 11 | 3.00 | 33.00 | GST |
| 4-201 | CAR01 | Car charger | 3 | 35.00 | 105.00 | GST |
| 4-201 | HAN01 | Hands-free kit | 1 | 70.00 | 70.00 | GST |
| 4-101 | V-727 | Vodingwell 727 phone | 5 | 920.00 | 4600.00 | GST |
| 4-101 | V-443 | Vodingwell 443 phone | 2 | 260.00 | 520.00 | GST |
| | | | | Subtotal | 5328.00 | |
| | | | | GST | 532.80 | |
| | | Banked 2/10/X1 | | Total | 5860.80 | |

```
Deposit          Ψ  PSI
receipt             BANK

Date: 30 Sept. 20X1
Branch: Woodton
Account name: Marvellous Mobile
Phones
Account no.: 3423 7467
Details: Till receipts
(T1707)
Amount: $5860.80        Teller
                          AB
```

**Accounts**

| From: | Adam Wang |
|---|---|
| Sent: | 30 September 20X1 |
| To: | Accounts |
| Subject: | Interest earned on Investment account |

Hi

The investment account has earned $68.85 in interest for September X1. Please record this in the general journal.

Thanks, Adam

**Stocktake Sheet**
**As at 30 September 20X1**

| Code | Description | Qty counted | As per inventory cards | Difference |
|---|---|---|---|---|
| BLI01 | Bling/jewellery | 69 | | |
| CAR01 | Car charger | 6 | | |
| COV01 | Phone covers | 4 | | |
| HAN01 | Hands-free kit | 12 | | |
| V-727 | Vodingwell 727 | 4 | | |
| V-443 | Vodingwell 443 | 4 | | |

MARVELLOUS MOBILE PHONES: A Manual Accounting Practice Set

---

**Checklist for End-of-Month Journals**

**30 September 20X1**

| | | |
|---|---|---|
| 1. | Journal Stocktake Adjustments | _____ |
| 2. | Accrue wages of $1916.67 | _____ |
| 3. | Record Superannuation Expense of 9% for **Paid** September Wages | _____ |
| 4. | Record Depreciation Expense * (Do not depreciate the printer) | _____ |
| 5. | Expense appropriate amount of | |
| | —Prepaid Insurance * | |
| | —Prepaid Advertising * | _____ |
| 6. | Adjust Allowance for Doubtful Debts to 2% of Accounts Receivable (rounded to the nearest cent) | _____ |

---

*\* See chapter 2, Account-keeping procedures and policies*

© 2011 Cengage Australia Pty Ltd

| BANK RECONCILIATION As at 31 August 20X1 | | | | |
|---|---|---|---|---|
| Balance as per bank statement | | | 7812.06 | Cr |
| ADD: Deposits not yet credited by bank | | | 0.00 | |
| | | | 7812.06 | |
| | Cheque no. | | | |
| LESS: Unpresented cheques | 2066 | 142.55 | | |
| | 2067 | 550.00 | 692.55 | |
| Balance as per Cash at Bank | | | 7119.51 | Dr |

## Ψ  PSI BANK

**Bank Statement**

Account number 3423 7467

Marvellous Mobiles
PO Box 8022
Woodton WA 6008

Enquiries: 14 14 14
www.psi.com.au

| Date 20X1 | Transaction details | Withdrawals ($) | Deposits ($) | Balance ($) | |
|---|---|---|---|---|---|
| 01/09 | Opening Balance | | | 7,812.06 | Cr |
| | Cheque 2066 | 142.55 | | 7,669.51 | |
| | Cheque 2067 | 550.00 | | 7,119.51 | |
| 04/09 | Deposit | | 961.40 | 8,080.91 | |
| 06/09 | Cheque 2070 | 660.00 | | 7,420.91 | |
| | EFT 334 A. Wang wages | 1,480.00 | | 5,940.91 | |
| | EFT 339 T. Cornwell wages | 470.00 | | 5,470.91 | |
| 7/09 | Deposit | | 303.60 | 5,774.51 | |
| | Cheque 2069 | 51.00 | | 5,723.51 | |
| 08/09 | Cheque 2068 | 222.31 | | 5,501.20 | |
| 11/09 | Deposit | | 1,916.20 | 7,417.40 | |
| 12/09 | Deposit | | 290.40 | 7,707.80 | |
| 13/09 | Deposit | | 4,753.98 | 12,461.78 | |
| 14/09 | Deposit | | 1,945.90 | 14,407.68 | |
| 18/09 | Deposit | | 2,290.20 | 16,697.88 | |
| 19/09 | Cheque 2071 | 3,981.45 | | 12,716.43 | |
| 20/09 | EFT | 1,480.00 | | 11,236.43 | |
| | EFT | 470.00 | | 10,766.43 | |
| | Deposit | | 9,507.96 | 20,274.39 | |
| 21/09 | Cheque 2072 | 223.30 | | 20,051.09 | |
| | Cheque 2073 | 465.52 | | 19,585.57 | |
| | Deposit | | 1,020.80 | 20,606.37 | |
| 25/09 | Deposit | | 3,011.80 | 23,618.17 | |
| 26/09 | Deposit | | 506.00 | 24,124.17 | |
| 29/09 | Cheque 2074 | 3,103.65 | | 21,020.52 | |
| | Cheque 2076 | 928.40 | | 20,092.12 | |
| | Cheque 2075 | 414.00 | | 19,678.12 | |
| | Cheque 2077 | 112.20 | | 19,565.92 | |
| | BPAY | 2,672.00 | | 16,893.92 | |
| 30/09 | DD Bank Loan Interest | 200.00 | | 16,693.92 | |
| 30/09 | Bank Fees | 6.50 | | 16,687.42 | |
| | TOTALS this page | 17,632.88 | 26,508.24 | | |

# CHAPTER 5
# General Ledger accounts

## Assets

### Cheque Account
Account no. 1-101

| Date 20X1 | | Description | Post ref. | Debit | Credit | Balance |
|---|---|---|---|---|---|---|
| | | | | | | Dr |
| | | | | | | |
| | | | | | | |
| | | | | | | |
| | | | | | | |

### Investment Account
Account no. 1-102

| Date 20X1 | | Description | Post ref. | Debit | Credit | Balance |
|---|---|---|---|---|---|---|
| | | | | | | Dr |
| | | | | | | |
| | | | | | | |

### Petty Cash
Account no. 1-120

| Date 20X1 | | Description | Post ref. | Debit | Credit | Balance |
|---|---|---|---|---|---|---|
| | | | | | | Dr |

### Accounts Receivable
Account no. 1-201

| Date 20X1 | | Description | Post ref. | Debit | Credit | Balance |
|---|---|---|---|---|---|---|
| | | | | | | Dr |
| | | | | | | |
| | | | | | | |
| | | | | | | |
| | | | | | | |
| | | | | | | |
| | | | | | | |

## Allowance Doubtful Debts                    Account no. 1-202

| Date 20X1 | | Description | Post ref. | Debit | Credit | Balance |
|---|---|---|---|---|---|---|
| | | | | | | Cr |
| | | | | | | |

## Merchandise Inventory                      Account no. 1-300

| Date 20X1 | | Description | Post ref. | Debit | Credit | Balance |
|---|---|---|---|---|---|---|
| | | | | | | Dr |
| | | | | | | |
| | | | | | | |
| | | | | | | |
| | | | | | | |
| | | | | | | |
| | | | | | | |
| | | | | | | |

## GST Paid                                    Account no. 1-400

| Date 20X1 | | Description | Post ref. | Debit | Credit | Balance |
|---|---|---|---|---|---|---|
| | | | | | | Dr |
| | | | | | | |
| | | | | | | |
| | | | | | | |
| | | | | | | |
| | | | | | | |
| | | | | | | |
| | | | | | | |
| | | | | | | |

## Prepaid Insurance                           Account no. 1-500

| Date 20X1 | | Description | Post ref. | Debit | Credit | Balance |
|---|---|---|---|---|---|---|
| | | | | | | Dr |
| | | | | | | |

## Prepaid Advertising                         Account no. 1-510

| Date 20X1 | | Description | Post ref. | Debit | Credit | Balance |
|---|---|---|---|---|---|---|
| | | | | | | Dr |
| | | | | | | |

## Office Equipment at Cost                    Account no. 1-701

| Date 20X1 | | Description | Post ref. | Debit | Credit | Balance |
|---|---|---|---|---|---|---|
| | | | | | | Dr |
| | | | | | | |
| | | | | | | |

## Office Equipment Accum. Dep'n            Account no. 1-702

| Date 20X1 | | Description | Post ref. | Debit | Credit | Balance |
|---|---|---|---|---|---|---|
| | | | | | | Cr |
| | | | | | | |
| | | | | | | |

## Shop Furniture /Fix at Cost               Account no. 1-801

| Date 20X1 | | Description | Post ref. | Debit | Credit | Balance |
|---|---|---|---|---|---|---|
| | | | | | | Dr |
| | | | | | | |
| | | | | | | |

## Shop Furniture/Fix – Accum. Dep'n        Account no. 1-802

| Date 20X1 | | Description | Post ref. | Debit | Credit | Balance |
|---|---|---|---|---|---|---|
| | | | | | | Cr |
| | | | | | | |
| | | | | | | |

# Liabilities and equity

## Accounts Payable — Account no. 2-120

| Date 20X1 | Description | Post ref. | Debit | Credit | Balance |
|---|---|---|---|---|---|
| | | | | | Cr |
| | | | | | |
| | | | | | |
| | | | | | |
| | | | | | |
| | | | | | |
| | | | | | |

## GST Collected — Account no. 2-131

| Date 20X1 | Description | Post ref. | Debit | Credit | Balance |
|---|---|---|---|---|---|
| | | | | | Cr |
| | | | | | |
| | | | | | |
| | | | | | |
| | | | | | |

## Superannuation Payable — Account no. 2-141

| Date 20X1 | Description | Post ref. | Debit | Credit | Balance |
|---|---|---|---|---|---|
| | | | | | Cr |
| | | | | | |
| | | | | | |

## PAYG Withholding Payable — Account no. 2-142

| Date 20X1 | Description | Post ref. | Debit | Credit | Balance |
|---|---|---|---|---|---|
| | | | | | Cr |
| | | | | | |

## Accrued Wages — Account no. 2-150

| Date 20X1 | Description | Post ref. | Debit | Credit | Balance |
|---|---|---|---|---|---|
| | | | | | Cr |
| | | | | | |

## Bank Loans                                    Account no. 2-210

| Date 20X1 | | Description | Post | Debit | Credit | Balance |
|---|---|---|---|---|---|---|
| | | | | | | Cr |

## Owner Equity – Adam Wang                      Account no. 3-101

| Date 20X1 | | Description | Post ref. | Debit | Credit | Balance |
|---|---|---|---|---|---|---|
| | | | | | | Cr |

## Owner Drawings – Adam Wang                    Account no. 3-102

| Date 20X1 | | Description | Post ref. | Debit | Credit | Balance |
|---|---|---|---|---|---|---|
| | | | | | | Dr |

## Income Summary                                Account no. 3-200

| Date 20X1 | | Description | Post ref. | Debit | Credit | Balance |
|---|---|---|---|---|---|---|
| | | | | | | Cr |
| | | | | | | |
| | | | | | | |
| | | | | | | |

# Income

## Sales Mobile Phones                                    Account no. 4-101

| Date 20X1 | | Description | Post ref. | Debit | Credit | Balance |
|---|---|---|---|---|---|---|
| | | | | | | |
| | | | | | | |
| | | | | | | |
| | | | | | | |

## Sales Accessories                                    Account no. 4-201

| Date 20X1 | | Description | Post ref. | Debit | Credit | Balance |
|---|---|---|---|---|---|---|
| | | | | | | |
| | | | | | | |
| | | | | | | |
| | | | | | | |

## Sales Discounts                                    Account no. 4-701

| Date 20X1 | | Description | Post ref. | Debit | Credit | Balance |
|---|---|---|---|---|---|---|
| | | | | | | |
| | | | | | | |
| | | | | | | |
| | | | | | | |

## Sales Returns                                    Account no. 4-801

| Date 20X1 | | Description | Post ref. | Debit | Credit | Balance |
|---|---|---|---|---|---|---|
| | | | | | | |
| | | | | | | |
| | | | | | | |

## Interest Received                                    Account no. 4-901

| Date 20X1 | | Description | Post ref. | Debit | Credit | Balance |
|---|---|---|---|---|---|---|
| | | | | | | |
| | | | | | | |
| | | | | | | |

# Cost of goods sold

## COGS Mobile Phones

**Account no. 5-101**

| Date 20X1 | | Description | Post ref. | Debit | Credit | Balance |
|---|---|---|---|---|---|---|
| | | | | | | |
| | | | | | | |
| | | | | | | |

## COGS Accessories

**Account no. 5-201**

| Date 20X1 | | Description | Post ref. | Debit | Credit | Balance |
|---|---|---|---|---|---|---|
| | | | | | | |
| | | | | | | |
| | | | | | | |

## Purchase Discount/Return

**Account no. 5-701**

| Date 20X1 | | Description | Post ref. | Debit | Credit | Balance |
|---|---|---|---|---|---|---|
| | | | | | | |
| | | | | | | |
| | | | | | | |

## Freight Paid

**Account no. 5-910**

| Date 20X1 | | Description | Post ref. | Debit | Credit | Balance |
|---|---|---|---|---|---|---|
| | | | | | | |
| | | | | | | |
| | | | | | | |

## Stock Adjustments

**Account no. 5-920**

| Date 20X1 | | Description | Post ref. | Debit | Credit | Balance |
|---|---|---|---|---|---|---|
| | | | | | | |
| | | | | | | |
| | | | | | | |

# Expenses

## Advertising Expense                                    Account no. 6-101

| Date 20X1 | | Description | Post ref. | Debit | Credit | Balance |
|---|---|---|---|---|---|---|
| | | | | | | |
| | | | | | | |

## Accounting/Legal                                    Account no. 6-102

| Date 20X1 | | Description | Post ref. | Debit | Credit | Balance |
|---|---|---|---|---|---|---|
| | | | | | | |
| | | | | | | |

## Bank Charges                                    Account no. 6-103

| Date 20X1 | | Description | Post ref. | Debit | Credit | Balance |
|---|---|---|---|---|---|---|
| | | | | | | |
| | | | | | | |

## Depreciation Expense                                    Account no. 6-111

| Date 20X1 | | Description | Post ref. | Debit | Credit | Balance |
|---|---|---|---|---|---|---|
| | | | | | | |
| | | | | | | |

## Electricity                                    Account no. 6-211

| Date 20X1 | | Description | Post ref. | Debit | Credit | Balance |
|---|---|---|---|---|---|---|
| | | | | | | |
| | | | | | | |

## Insurance Expense                                    Account no. 6-212

| Date 20X1 | | Description | Post ref. | Debit | Credit | Balance |
|---|---|---|---|---|---|---|
| | | | | | | |
| | | | | | | |

## Donations                                                    Account no. 6-213

| Date 20X1 | | Description | Post ref. | Debit | Credit | Balance |
|---|---|---|---|---|---|---|
| | | | | | | |
| | | | | | | |

## Rent                                                          Account no. 6-214

| Date 20X1 | | Description | Post ref. | Debit | Credit | Balance |
|---|---|---|---|---|---|---|
| | | | | | | |
| | | | | | | |

## Stationery/Printing                                          Account no. 6-215

| Date 20X1 | | Description | Post ref. | Debit | Credit | Balance |
|---|---|---|---|---|---|---|
| | | | | | | |
| | | | | | | |
| | | | | | | |

## Telephone/Internet                                           Account no. 6-216

| Date 20X1 | | Description | Post ref. | Debit | Credit | Balance |
|---|---|---|---|---|---|---|
| | | | | | | |
| | | | | | | |

## Postage                                                       Account no. 6-217

| Date 20X1 | | Description | Post ref. | Debit | Credit | Balance |
|---|---|---|---|---|---|---|
| | | | | | | |
| | | | | | | |

## Wages Payable                                                 Account no. 6-301

| Date 20X1 | | Description | Post ref. | Debit | Credit | Balance |
|---|---|---|---|---|---|---|
| | | | | | | |
| | | | | | | |
| | | | | | | |

## Superannuation Expense                         Account no. 6-302

| Date 20X1 | | Description | Post ref. | Debit | Credit | Balance |
|---|---|---|---|---|---|---|
| | | | | | | |
| | | | | | | |
| | | | | | | |

## Staff Amenities                               Account no. 6-303

| Date 20X1 | | Description | Post ref. | Debit | Credit | Balance |
|---|---|---|---|---|---|---|
| | | | | | | |
| | | | | | | |
| | | | | | | |

## Interest Expense                              Account no. 6-901

| Date 20X1 | | Description | Post ref. | Debit | Credit | Balance |
|---|---|---|---|---|---|---|
| | | | | | | |
| | | | | | | |
| | | | | | | |

## Bad/Doubtful Debt Expense                     Account no. 6-902

| Date 20X1 | | Description | Post ref. | Debit | Credit | Balance |
|---|---|---|---|---|---|---|
| | | | | | | |
| | | | | | | |
| | | | | | | |

# General Journal

| Date | | Description | Post | Debit | Credit |
|---|---|---|---|---|---|
| | | | | | |
| | | | | | |
| | | | | | |
| | | | | | |
| | | | | | |
| | | | | | |
| | | | | | |
| | | | | | |
| | | | | | |
| | | | | | |
| | | | | | |
| | | | | | |
| | | | | | |
| | | | | | |
| | | | | | |
| | | | | | |
| | | | | | |
| | | | | | |
| | | | | | |
| | | | | | |
| | | | | | |
| | | | | | |
| | | | | | |
| | | | | | |
| | | | | | |
| | | | | | |
| | | | | | |
| | | | | | |
| | | | | | |
| | | | | | |
| | | | | | |
| | | | | | |
| | | | | | |
| | | | | | |
| | | | | | |
| | | | | | |
| | | | | | |

# General Journal

| Date | | Description | Post | Debit | Credit |
|---|---|---|---|---|---|
| | | | | | |

# General Journal

| Date | | Description | Post | Debit | Credit |
|---|---|---|---|---|---|
| | | | | | |
| | | | | | |
| | | | | | |
| | | | | | |
| | | | | | |
| | | | | | |
| | | | | | |
| | | | | | |
| | | | | | |
| | | | | | |
| | | | | | |
| | | | | | |
| | | | | | |
| | | | | | |
| | | | | | |
| | | | | | |
| | | | | | |
| | | | | | |
| | | | | | |
| | | | | | |
| | | | | | |
| | | | | | |
| | | | | | |
| | | | | | |
| | | | | | |
| | | | | | |
| | | | | | |
| | | | | | |
| | | | | | |
| | | | | | |
| | | | | | |
| | | | | | |
| | | | | | |
| | | | | | |
| | | | | | |
| | | | | | |
| | | | | | |
| | | | | | |
| | | | | | |

# CHAPTER 6
# Special journals

**Purchases Journal**

| Date | | Suppliers | Terms | Post | Inventory Dr | Freight Paid Dr | GST Paid Dr | Accounts Payable Cr |
|---|---|---|---|---|---|---|---|---|
| | | | | | | | | |
| | | | | | | | | |
| | | | | | | | | |
| | | | | | | | | |
| | | | | | | | | |
| | | | | | | | | |
| | | | | | | | | |
| | | | | | | | | |
| | | | | | | | | |
| | | | | | | | | |

## Sales Journal

| Date 20X1 | Description | Post ref. | Invoice no. | Sales Mob Phones Cr | Sales Accessories Cr | GST Collected Cr | Accounts Rec. Dr | COGS Mob. Phones Dr/Cr | COGS Accessories Dr/Cr |
|---|---|---|---|---|---|---|---|---|---|
| | | | | | | | | | |
| | | | | | | | | | |

# Cash Receipts Journal

| Date 20X1 | Description | Post ref. | Sales invoice No. | Cash at Bank Dr | Accounts Rec. Cr | Sales Mob. Phones Cr | Sales Access Cr | Sales Discounts Dr | GST Collected Cr | COGS Mob. Phones | COGS Accessories Dr/Cr |
|---|---|---|---|---|---|---|---|---|---|---|---|
| | | | | | | | | | | | |
| | | | | | | | | | | | |

## Cash Payments Journal

| Date 20X1 | Description | Post ref. | Cheque no. | Cheque Account Cr | Accounts Payable Dr | Purchase Discount Cr | Salaries Dr | PAYG Withhold Cr | Other accounts | | GST Paid Dr |
|---|---|---|---|---|---|---|---|---|---|---|---|
| | | | | | | | | | Acc no. | Dr | |
| | | | | | | | | | | | |
| | | | | | | | | | | | |
| | | | | | | | | | | | |
| | | | | | | | | | | | |
| | | | | | | | | | | | |
| | | | | | | | | | | | |
| | | | | | | | | | | | |
| | | | | | | | | | | | |
| | | | | | | | | | | | |
| | | | | | | | | | | | |
| | | | | | | | | | | | |
| | | | | | | | | | | | |

# Petty Cash Book

| Date 20X1 | | Description | Vchr no. | Receipts | Payments | Postage | Staff Amens | Stationery | Other accounts | | GST Paid |
|---|---|---|---|---|---|---|---|---|---|---|---|
| | | | | | | | | | Acc no. | Amount | |
| Aug. | 31 | Balance b/d | | 57.45 | | | | | | | |
| | | Reimburse Chq 2066 | | 142.55 | | | | | | | |
| | | | | | | | | | | | |
| | | | | | | | | | | | |
| | | | | | | | | | | | |
| | | | | | | | | | | | |
| | | | | | | | | | | | |
| | | | | | | | | | | | |
| | | | | | | | | | | | |
| | | | | | | | | | | | |
| | | | | | | | | | | | |
| | | | | | | | | | | | |
| | | | | | | | | | | | |
| | | | | | | | | | | | |

# CHAPTER 7
# Subsidiary Ledgers

## Accounts Receivable Subsidiary Ledger

**Ableton University**                                                    Account no. ABE01

| Date | Description | Post ref. | Debit | Credit | Balance |
|------|-------------|-----------|-------|--------|---------|
|      |             |           |       |        |         |
|      |             |           |       |        |         |
|      |             |           |       |        |         |

**Magic Mop**                                                            Account no. MAG01

| Date | Description | Post ref. | Debit | Credit | Balance |
|------|-------------|-----------|-------|--------|---------|
|      |             |           |       |        |         |
|      |             |           |       |        |         |

**Mia Mio NL**                                                           Account no. MIA01

| Date | Description | Post ref. | Debit | Credit | Balance |
|------|-------------|-----------|-------|--------|---------|
|      |             |           |       |        |         |
|      |             |           |       |        |         |

**Mobilelot Ableton University**                                         Account no. MOB01

| Date | Description | Post ref. | Debit | Credit | Balance |
|------|-------------|-----------|-------|--------|---------|
|      |             |           |       |        |         |
|      |             |           |       |        |         |
|      |             |           |       |        |         |
|      |             |           |       |        |         |

**Mobilelot Woodton TAFE**                                               Account no. MOB02

| Date | Description | Post ref. | Debit | Credit | Balance |
|------|-------------|-----------|-------|--------|---------|
|      |             |           |       |        |         |
|      |             |           |       |        |         |
|      |             |           |       |        |         |
|      |             |           |       |        |         |

# Accounts Payable Subsidiary Ledger

## Electricity Co.                                        Account no. ELE01

| Date | | Description | Post ref. | Debit | Credit | Balance |
|---|---|---|---|---|---|---|
| | | | | | | |
| | | | | | | |

## Fone Bling                                            Account no. FON01

| Date | | Description | Post ref. | Debit | Credit | Balance |
|---|---|---|---|---|---|---|
| | | | | | | |
| | | | | | | |

## Phone Bits                                            Account no. PHO01

| Date | | Description | Post ref. | Debit | Credit | Balance |
|---|---|---|---|---|---|---|
| | | | | | | |
| | | | | | | |
| | | | | | | |
| | | | | | | |

## Telpho Communications                                 Account no. TEL01

| Date | | Description | Post ref. | Debit | Credit | Balance |
|---|---|---|---|---|---|---|
| | | | | | | |
| | | | | | | |
| | | | | | | |
| | | | | | | |

## Vodingwell                                            Account no. VOD01

| Date | | Description | Post ref. | Debit | Credit | Balance |
|---|---|---|---|---|---|---|
| | | | | | | |
| | | | | | | |
| | | | | | | |
| | | | | | | |
| | | | | | | |

## Woodton Shopping Centre                               Account no. WOO01

| Date | | Description | Post ref. | Debit | Credit | Balance |
|---|---|---|---|---|---|---|
| | | | | | | |
| | | | | | | |
| | | | | | | |

# CHAPTER 8
# Perpetual inventory cards

Item no. **BLI01**

Description: **Bling/jewellery**

| Date 20X1 | Particulars | In | | | Out | | | Balance | | |
|---|---|---|---|---|---|---|---|---|---|---|
| | | Qty | Unit cost | Total cost | Qty | Unit cost | Total cost | Qty | Unit cost | Total |
| | Opening balance | | | | | | | 149 | 1.50 | 223.50 |
| | | | | | | | | | | |
| | | | | | | | | | | |
| | | | | | | | | | | |
| | | | | | | | | | | |
| | | | | | | | | | | |
| | | | | | | | | | | |
| | | | | | | | | | | |
| | | | | | | | | | | |
| | | | | | | | | | | |
| | | | | | | | | | | |
| | | | | | | | | | | |
| | | | | | | | | | | |

Item no. **CAR01**

Description: **Car charger**

| Date | Particulars | In | | | Out | | | Balance | | |
|---|---|---|---|---|---|---|---|---|---|---|
| 20X1 | | Qty | Unit cost | Total cost | Qty | Unit cost | Total cost | Qty | Unit cost | Total |
| | Opening balance | | | | | | | 16 | 14.00 | 224.00 |
| | | | | | | | | | | |
| | | | | | | | | | | |
| | | | | | | | | | | |
| | | | | | | | | | | |
| | | | | | | | | | | |
| | | | | | | | | | | |
| | | | | | | | | | | |

Item no. **COV01**

Description: **Phone covers**

| Date 20X1 | Particulars | In | | | Out | | | Balance | | |
|---|---|---|---|---|---|---|---|---|---|---|
| | | Qty | Unit cost | Total cost | Qty | Unit cost | Total cost | Qty | Unit cost | Total |
| | Opening balance | | | | | | | 26 | 13.00 | 338.00 |
| | | | | | | | | | | |
| | | | | | | | | | | |
| | | | | | | | | | | |
| | | | | | | | | | | |
| | | | | | | | | | | |
| | | | | | | | | | | |
| | | | | | | | | | | |
| | | | | | | | | | | |

Item no. **HAN01**

Description: **Hands-free kit**

| Date 20X1 | Particulars | In | | | Out | | | Balance | | |
|---|---|---|---|---|---|---|---|---|---|---|
| | | Qty | Unit cost | Total cost | Qty | Unit cost | Total cost | Qty | Unit cost | Total |
| | Opening balance | | | | | | | 10 | 35.00 | 350.00 |
| | | | | | | | | | | |
| | | | | | | | | | | |
| | | | | | | | | | | |
| | | | | | | | | | | |
| | | | | | | | | | | |
| | | | | | | | | | | |
| | | | | | | | | | | |
| | | | | | | | | | | |

Item no. **V-443**

Description: **Vodingwell 443 phone**

| Date 20X1 | Particulars | In | | | Out | | | Balance | | |
|---|---|---|---|---|---|---|---|---|---|---|
| | | Qty | Unit cost | Total cost | Qty | Unit cost | Total cost | Qty | Unit cost | Total |
| | Opening balance | | | | | | | 6 | 130.00 | 780.00 |
| | | | | | | | | | | |
| | | | | | | | | | | |
| | | | | | | | | | | |
| | | | | | | | | | | |
| | | | | | | | | | | |
| | | | | | | | | | | |
| | | | | | | | | | | |

Item no. **V-727**

Description: **Vodingwell 727 phone**

| Date | Particulars | In | | | Out | | | Balance | | |
|---|---|---|---|---|---|---|---|---|---|---|
| 20X1 | | Qty | Unit cost | Total cost | Qty | Unit cost | Total cost | Qty | Unit cost | Total |
| | Opening balance | | | | | | | 22 | 580.00 | 12,760.00 |
| | | | | | | | | | | |
| | | | | | | | | | | |
| | | | | | | | | | | |
| | | | | | | | | | | |
| | | | | | | | | | | |
| | | | | | | | | | | |
| | | | | | | | | | | |
| | | | | | | | | | | |
| | | | | | | | | | | |

# CHAPTER 9
# Financial reports and schedules

## Schedules for September X1

| BANK RECONCILIATION | | | |
|---|---|---|---|
| As at 30 September 20X1 | | | |
| Balance as per bank statement | | | Cr |
| **ADD:** Deposits not yet credited by bank | | | |
| | Cheque no. | Amount | |
| **LESS:** Unpresented cheques | | | |
| Balance as per Cash at Bank | | | Dr |

| Accounts Receivable | | | | |
|---|---|---|---|---|
| As at 30 September 20X1 | | | | |
| **Code** | **Customer** | **Invoice date** | **Invoice no.** | **Amount** |
| | | | | |
| | | | | |
| | | | | |
| 1-201 | Accounts Receivable Control | | | |

| Accounts Payable | | | | |
|---|---|---|---|---|
| As at 30 September 20X1 | | | | |
| **Code** | **Supplier** | **Invoice date** | **Invoice no.** | **Amount** |
| | | | | |
| | | | | |
| 2-120 | Accounts Payable Control | | | |

| | **Inventory Schedule**<br>**As at 30 September 20X1** | | |
|---|---|---|---|
| *Code* | *Description* | *Qty* | *Amount* |
| BLI01 | Phone Bling/jewellery | | |
| CAR01 | Car charger | | |
| COV01 | Phone covers | | |
| HAN01 | Hands-free kit | | |
| V-727 | Vodingwell 727 | | |
| V-443 | Vodingwell 443 | | |
| 1-300 | Inventory Control | | |

MARVELLOUS MOBILE PHONES: A Manual Accounting Practice Set

# Worksheet for September X1

| Account Code | Account | Trial Balance | | Adjustments | | Adjusted Trial Balance | | Income Statement | | Balance Sheet | |
|---|---|---|---|---|---|---|---|---|---|---|---|
| | | Dr | Cr | Dr | Cr | Dr | Cr | Dr | Cr | Dr | Cr |
| 1-101 | Cheque Account | | | | | | | | | | |
| 1-102 | Investment Account | | | | | | | | | | |
| 1-120 | Petty Cash | | | | | | | | | | |
| 1-201 | Accounts Receivable | | | | | | | | | | |
| 1-202 | Allow. Doubtful Debts | | | | | | | | | | |
| 1-300 | Merchandise Inventory | | | | | | | | | | |
| 1-400 | GST Paid | | | | | | | | | | |
| 1-500 | Prepaid Insurance | | | | | | | | | | |
| 1-510 | Prepaid Advertising | | | | | | | | | | |
| 1-701 | Office Equip. at Cost | | | | | | | | | | |
| 1-702 | Office Equip. Accum. Dep'n | | | | | | | | | | |
| 1-801 | Shop Furn./Fix. at Cost | | | | | | | | | | |
| 1-802 | Shop Furn./Fix. Accum. Dep'n | | | | | | | | | | |
| 2-120 | Accounts Payable | | | | | | | | | | |
| 2-131 | GST Collected | | | | | | | | | | |
| 2-141 | Superannuation Payable | | | | | | | | | | |
| 2-142 | PAYG Withholding Payable | | | | | | | | | | |
| 2-150 | Accrued Wages | | | | | | | | | | |
| 2-210 | Bank Loan | | | | | | | | | | |
| 3-101 | Owner Equity – Adam Wang | | | | | | | | | | |
| 3-102 | Owner Drawings – Adam Wang | | | | | | | | | | |
| 3-200 | Income Summary | | | | | | | | | | |
| 4-101 | Sales – Mobile Phones | | | | | | | | | | |
| 4-201 | Sales – Accessories | | | | | | | | | | |
| 4-701 | Sales Discounts | | | | | | | | | | |

© 2011 Cengage Australia Pty Ltd

| Account Code | Account | Trial Balance | | Adjustments | | Adjusted Trial Balance | | Income Statement | | Balance Sheet | |
|---|---|---|---|---|---|---|---|---|---|---|---|
| | | Dr | Cr | Dr | Cr | Dr | Cr | Dr | Cr | Dr | Cr |
| 4-801 | Sales Returns | | | | | | | | | | |
| 4-901 | Interest Received | | | | | | | | | | |
| 5-101 | COGS Mobile Phones | | | | | | | | | | |
| 5-201 | COGS Accessories | | | | | | | | | | |
| 5-701 | Purchase Discount/Return | | | | | | | | | | |
| 5-910 | Freight Paid | | | | | | | | | | |
| 5-920 | Stock Adjustments | | | | | | | | | | |
| 6-101 | Advertising | | | | | | | | | | |
| 6-102 | Accounting/Legal | | | | | | | | | | |
| 6-103 | Bank Charges | | | | | | | | | | |
| 6-111 | Depreciation Expense | | | | | | | | | | |
| 6-211 | Electricity | | | | | | | | | | |
| 6-212 | Insurance | | | | | | | | | | |
| 6-213 | Donations | | | | | | | | | | |
| 6-214 | Rent | | | | | | | | | | |
| 6-215 | Stationery/Printing | | | | | | | | | | |
| 6-216 | Telephone/Internet | | | | | | | | | | |
| 6-217 | Postage | | | | | | | | | | |
| 6-301 | Wages Expense | | | | | | | | | | |
| 6-302 | Superannuation Expense | | | | | | | | | | |
| 6-303 | Staff Amenities | | | | | | | | | | |
| 6-901 | Interest Expense | | | | | | | | | | |
| 6-902 | Bad/Doubtful Debt Expense | | | | | | | | | | |
| | | | | | | | | | | | |
| | | | | | | | | | | | |
| | | | | | | | | | | | |

**Marvellous Mobile Phones**
**Income Statement**
**September 20X1**

| | |
|---|---|
| **Income** | |
| Sales – Mobile Phones | |
| Sales – Accessories | |
| Sales Discounts | |
| Sales Returns | |
| Interest Received | |
| **TOTAL INCOME** | |
| **Cost of Sales** | |
| COGS – Mobile Phones | |
| COGS – Accessories | |
| Purchase Discounts/Returns | |
| Freight Paid | |
| Stock Adjustments | |
| **TOTAL COST OF SALES** | |
| **GROSS PROFIT** | |
| | |
| **Expenses** | |
| Advertising Expense | |
| Accounting/Legal | |
| Bank Charges | |
| Depreciation Expense | |
| Electricity | |
| Insurance Expense | |
| Donations | |
| Rent | |
| Stationery/Printing | |
| Telephone/Internet | |
| Postage | |
| Wages Expense | |
| Superannuation Expense | |
| Staff Amenities | |
| Interest Expense | |
| Bad/Doubtful Debt Expense | |
| **TOTAL EXPENSES** | |
| | |
| **NET PROFIT/(LOSS)** | |

**Marvellous Mobile Phones**
**Balance Sheet**
**As at 30 September 20X1**

**ASSETS**

Cheque Account

Investment Account

Petty Cash

Accounts Receivable

Allowance for Doubtful Debts

Net Accounts Receivable

Merchandise Inventory

GST Paid

Prepaid Insurance

Prepaid Advertising

Office Equip. at Cost

Office Equip. Accum. Dep.

Total Office Equipment

Shop Furn./Fix. at Cost

Shop Furn./Fix. Accum. Dep.

Total Shop Furn./Fixtures

**TOTAL ASSETS**


**LIABILITIES**

Accounts Payable

GST Collected

Superannuation Payable

PAYG Withholding Payable

Accrued Wages

Bank Loans

**TOTAL LIABILITIES**

**NET ASSETS**


**EQUITY**

Owner Equity – Adam Wang

Drawings – Adam Wang

Income Summary

**TOTAL EQUITY**

**Marvellous Mobile Phones**

**Post-Closing Trial Balance**

**As at 30 September 20X1**

| | | DR | CR |
|---|---|---|---|
| 1-101 | Cheque Account PSI 7467 | | |
| 1-102 | Investment Account | | |
| 1-120 | Petty Cash | | |
| 1-201 | Accounts Receivable | | |
| 1-202 | Allowance Doubtful Debts | | |
| 1-300 | Merchandise Inventory | | |
| 1-400 | GST Paid | | |
| 1-500 | Prepaid Insurance | | |
| 1-510 | Prepaid Advertising | | |
| 1-701 | Office Equipment at Cost | | |
| 1-702 | Office Equipment Accum. Dep'n | | |
| 1-801 | Shop Furn./Fixtures at Cost | | |
| 1-802 | Shop Furn./Fix. Accum. Dep. | | |
| 2-120 | Accounts Payable | | |
| 2-131 | GST Collected | | |
| 2-141 | Superannuation Payable | | |
| 2-142 | PAYG Withholding Payable | | |
| 2-150 | Accrued Wages | | |
| 2-210 | Bank Loans | | |
| 3-101 | Owner Equity – A Wang | | |
| 3-102 | Owner Drawing – A Wang | | |
| 3-200 | Income Summary | | |
| | **TOTALS** | | |

# Congratulations!

You have now finished your practice set. You have now learned the basis of every accounting package.

# *ALSO AVAILABLE AT YOUR CAMPUS BOOKSTORE...*

Rita's Animal Refuge: A Manual and
Computerised Accounting  Practice Set
Using *MYOB Accounting Plus Version 19*

9780170190817

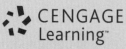